trainers

© Fitway Publishing, 2004.
Original editions in French, English, Castilian, Catalan, Italian

English language translation by Translate-A-Book, Oxford
Design and creation: GRAPH'M

ISBN: 2-7528-0064-9
Publisher code: T00064
Copyright registration: September 2004
Printed in Singapore by Tien Wah Press

www.fitwaypublishing.com
Fitway Publishing – 12, avenue d'Italie – 75627 Paris cedex 13

trainers

sandrine pereira

fitway.
publishing

Contents

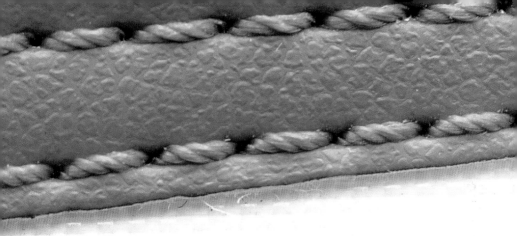

From stadium to street

Picture this if you will … an everyday scene in any fashion boutique in any trendy shopping mall. Under the same roof as creations of top designers and stylists, the shelves of a corner of the boutique are stocked with trainers. Things better suited – you might have thought – to street culture than to high fashion. On busy days, masses of keen buyers jostle with each other for the chance to examine the latest £100-plus hi-tech wonder, to see the fruits of the collaboration between some rising star of the fashion world and a leading manufacturer, or even to spot which celeb is wearing some recently repackaged classic tennis shoe.

In New York, Paris, London or Tokyo, it's the same story. Trainers bring them flocking in, the fashionistas as well as the local youth mafia. Trainers, sneakers, tennis or basketball shoes, call them what you like, sports shoes have undergone a staggering (r)evolution over the last four decades. Once only found in sports changing rooms, they have now entered the everyday world, worn by people of every age and social background. Whether chic, sophisticated, streetwise, or just plain cool, trainers are now as basic an item of clothing as jeans.

The US, Japan and France are full of trainer-maniacs. France, for example, recently hit sports shoe sales of almost 80 million pairs, representing a turnover of more than £1.8 billion. The real trainer fanatics are men, who buy 40 per cent of them – just for everyday wear.

The trainer brands quickly cottoned on to this widening of appeal beyond the sports tracks, and discovered how to exploit it. Their worldwide turnover is gi-normous: almost £8 million in 2002 alone. These multinationals, having responded to a change in the market place, now actually set the trends themselves each season, not least by increasing the number of technological innovations in each new line of footwear.

from changing-room
to wardrobe

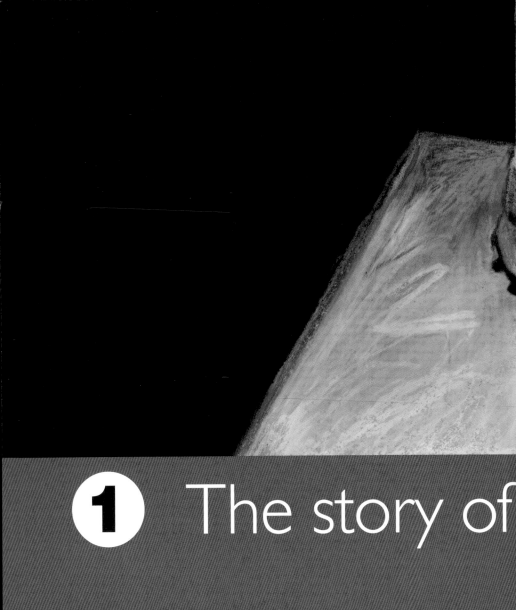

1 The story of

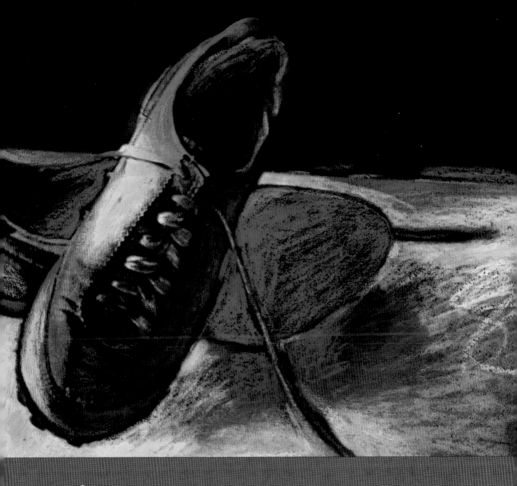

a shoe

Once upon a time …

To tell the extraordinary tale of the sports shoe or trainer we have to go back in time to around the sixteenth and seventeenth centuries, and it is a story that embraces the Old and New Worlds.

In South America, the Spanish conquistadors noticed a curious native Indian custom. After harvesting latex from rubber trees, the Indians used to rub a little of it on their feet, to protect their arches, heels and toes. In the same period, in the European courts, the privileged few were taking up real tennis, the fashionable sport of the day. To play it they wore rather uncomfortable dancing shoes made of felt. The approach to the game was genteel, then, and not fiercely competitive.

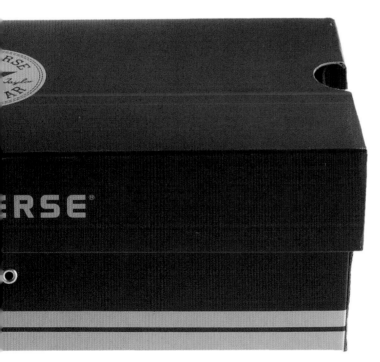

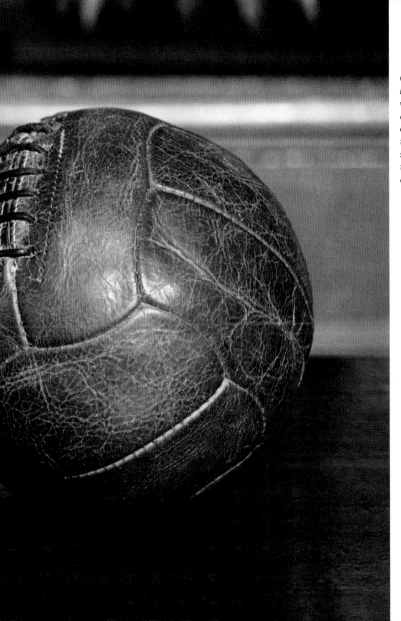

Omens of a revolution: a sole with studs, laces, and a high boot ... everything needed to make this sports shoe a really up-to-date trainer is already there.

It was not until a few centuries later that the South American Indian invention was adapted by the Europeans to give us the first modern sports shoes. For most of the nineteenth century, Brazil was the world's main rubber producer. Advances made in the eighteenth century had shown that liquefied latex could be poured into clay moulds, thus making it much more adaptable. It was dried in the smoke of palm nut fires; the nuts, when burnt, released large amounts of phenol and acetic acid, chemical elements that enabled the latex to be stabilised. The resulting rubber was then used to make shoe soles.

Trade between North America and Europe began to flourish in the 1820s. The first ships arrived from Brazil, loaded with rubber-soled shoes. Scientists and businessmen were among those who took a keen interest in this new material. They wanted to solve the main problems involved in its use, especially that of reducing the rubber's physical instability.

Soon, its wider potential was discovered. In 1823, a Scotsman called Mackintosh experimented with naphtha, which could dissolve latex quickly and cleanly. But it was only in 1839 that Charles Goodyear, a hardware-store owner from Philadelphia, perfected the vulcanisation process that led to mass production of the first 'tennis' shoes. This procedure

The latest basketball gear? No, the newest word in playground chic.

made it possible to heat the latex with sulphur and lead carbonate, so that the rubber could be manipulated easily. The final and decisive stage in its development was the invention of synthetic rubber in 1920 – the result of a rather complex chemical process.

In the early nineteenth century, however, the ankle boots then in fashion were the prototypes of what we now call trainers. Sport was no longer the absolute prerogative of the privileged few, even though it did remain almost exclusively so. To play tennis, their favourite game, aristocrats wore lace-up shoes with rubber or (worse) cord soles. Even then, fashion was a consideration; it was considered good form in polite society to adopt the appearance of a sportsman rather than to actually be one, and tennis parties were thought of as entertainment for the modern gentleman, rather than contests.

The development of a specific vocabulary for physical exercise was one indicator of the way in which attitudes to sport were developing. The term 'sneakers', for instance, is said to have appeared in England in 1875 as a description of croquet shoes, croquet being a popular game among high-society women.

Towards the end of the century, physical exercise began to be an important element in the curriculum at top schools, and

Sport is fashionable …
You can't argue with that!

It's only one step from super-refined Nikes to hi-tech designs.

it was here that the first sports clubs were started. Teachers instilled the notions of effort, team spirit and fair play (things had moved on since the days of duels with sword and pistol). Naturally, the clothes commonly worn at that time were soon considered outdated, as sportsmen realised they needed clothes, not so much to appear elegant, but to allow their bodies to move freely. Sportswear became increasingly less formal and more thought was put into making it more flexible, enabling games to be played at greater speed.

The first great leap forward

The beginning of the twentieth century saw a rapid increase in differing types of sports shoe: leather boots without laces, with bands of non-slip leather; moccasins with cloth heels; and side-buttoned shoes with leather soles, metal fittings, and punctured-felt meshes to allow the feet to breathe. The transformation was spectacular, and one reason for this was the opening up of sport to all levels of society. This was sparked off in 1896 when the first Olympic Games were held in Athens. The event, organised by Baron Pierre de

Fabric trainers and rubber soles,
all you need to be over the moon,
according to this ad!

RS

3290

3276

Coubertin, involved people from all over the world and enabled sport and sports equipment to take a giant leap forward. Things were to speed up during the course of the century, with the advent of the leisure society and the first workers' paid holidays. From now on, men and women started to look on athletes as role models, perfect incarnations of the notion of a 'pure soul in a pure body'.

Apart from the croquet shoe, invented in 1860, the first mass-market sports shoe was the 'Ked' (from 'kid', in the sense of child, and from '*pes, pedis*' the Latin word for foot). It was launched by U.S. Rubber, in 1917, sold at an affordable price, and was the first 'trainer' of the twentieth century. The ancestor of the basketball boot, the 'All Star', appeared for the first time in 1919. It had a dyed cloth upper and a rubber sole, sported a badge of stars on one side, and became an instant hit.

Although tennis began to be a more popular game lower down the social scale, in practice the leisured classes still dominated the sport. The famous clothes' designers of the period were well aware of this. In Paris, Coco Chanel, Jean Patou, and even Lanvin provided areas devoted to sports clothes and shoes in their elegant boutiques. Aesthetic considerations were not, however, a priority for industrial manufacturers. All they wanted was to improve the technical qualities of their shoes, and thus the performance of the professional sportsmen who caught the public's interest and admiration, and whose exploits the media relayed around the world. This marked the start of modern marketing. In Germany, Adi Hassler (later to found Adidas) began to make his mark. His first claim to fame was at the Berlin Olympics in 1936, when his shoes were worn by the black American athlete, Jesse Owens.

*Athletes are a gift
for people working
on brand awareness.*

First signs of a revolution

The American lifestyle did a lot to popularise trainers. First and foremost, they were a youth phenomenon. In the 1950s, the carefree attitude of the postwar period and new, young idols on screen, provided the ideal setting for young, carefree footwear. James Dean, Elvis Presley, the main characters in the film *West Side Story* (all wearing Converse shoes), and the cool rebel look they cultivated so successfully, influenced a whole generation. Already, in the 1930s and '40s, glamorous Hollywood stars such as Katharine Hepburn and Marlene Dietrich had become synonymous with elegance, often wearing masculine-looking suits and sports shoes. Elegant sportswear, in a way, helped launch their careers. A combination of highly competitive prices and the development of physical education and sports in schools also helped to make trainers trendy in the eyes of teenagers.

Don't get your ballet shoes out.
All you need for a perfect entrechat
is a good old pair of trainers.

Then the big manufacturers geared up to turn out sports shoes in huge quantities. They made use of the latest technological advances in order to improve athletic performance, but they also began to pay attention to image, strategically relaunching their best-selling models in innovative colours designed to win over a public eager for new products and seduced by the street appeal of the shoes. Fashion considerations began to compete with sporting ones. In fact, they were intimately connected, and each influenced the other. When a sport or pastime suddenly enjoys particular popularity, the manufacturers produce specially adapted models which will not only be suitable on the track but will also be good for everyday wear. In the 1960s, when jogging was all the rage and parks everywhere were packed with joggers, and fitness fanatic Jane Fonda was on every magazine cover, women wanted not only to be like Jane Fonda but to look like her and wear the same clothes. Public attitudes like this helped sportswear to evolve, and fashion designers in their turn reinterpreted it.

Nike as a fashion icon in a Saturday Night Fever *version.*

The year 1970 saw the blossoming of the Flower Power generation; it questioned the values of consumer society and wore trainers to reinforce its anti-establishment image. Celebrities jumped on the bandwagon and started wearing hip outfits, long hair and trainers. The decade heralded a golden age of the sports shoe, and new trainer brands made bids to outdo the old ones, such as 'Keds', Adidas, Converse, and P. F. Flyers. Nike made its first appearance in 1979.

Customised Flower Power trainers.

The logos are almost as important as the manufacturers' technical reputation.

This newcomer declared war on its predecessors with the Nike 'Air Concept', with soles containing cavities filled with pressurised gas. The advent of this air-cushioned version marked the beginning of a battle between manufacturers, who were anxious for market share on the one hand but also keen to be seen as innovative sports equipment developers on the other.

On the streets, two new phenomena had a profound effect on the trainer market: the wider acceptability of trainers, particularly in the workplace, and the advent of Hip Hop and rap culture. Teenagers were no longer the only ones wearing trainers away from running tracks and playgrounds. At the start of the '80s thousands of women in shoulder-padded suits were to be seen jogging briskly along the New York pavements towards their offices wearing a pair of Reebok

An aerobics class. Trendy in the 1980s, aerobics influenced fashion and put trainers in the public eye.

'Freestyles'. (Unusually here, Reebok was an English firm, although the key players were, at the time, German and American companies). This evolution in dress conventions was captured in the film *Working Girl*, inspired by the 1980 transport strike. The heroine of the film, played by Melanie Griffith, became an icon, an emblem of a time when the frontiers between leisure (aerobics was at its height and Reeboks were an indispensable necessity) and professional life were blurred, where there was still a fairly rigorously enforced code of rules governing appearance (when she reached her office, Melanie Griffith quickly changed into smart working shoes before entering the building). It is still a long way from the Dress-Down-Friday concept, which came in at the end of the '90s, permitting the wearing of casual wear and trainers in the office on the last day of the working week, but dress codes were in the process of changing.

An NBA basketball match. The players are role models and wear top-of-the-range versions which young people then rush out to buy.

During the 1980s the influence of the street grew as fast as that of the sports stadium, thanks mainly to Hip Hop. Rappers were a very fashion-conscious crowd, and based their look around sports gear, though not your average golfer, tennis player or footballer clothing. Instead, they took their inspiration from the players of the NBA (National Basketball Association). In 1986, Adidas formalised this link by their groundbreaking decision to sponsor the rap group, Run DMC. The group's song, *My Adidas*, was an international hit. This was a real publicity coup for the German company, which was suffering serious competition from Nike, who, the year before, had signed a contract with Michael Jordan, the most famous player in the history of the NBA. The highly successful Nike 'Air Jordan' (produced in 15 different versions) was one of the results of this tie-up, all sold at extremely high prices, and to young people, the main target market for branded trainers.

Trainers make their first appearance in top designers' fashion shows, from Jean-Paul Gaultier to Yohji Yamamoto.

In 1993 just three brands – Adidas, Nike and Reebok – were responsible for nearly 85 per cent of worldwide sales, with turnover in millions of dollars. Small-scale factories were now out of the question, and industrialisation started to reach incredible levels. Manufacturers relocated, mainly to South-East Asia, where more than 50 per cent of trainers were produced by the end of the '80s; the percentage increased steadily over the next decade. With the emergence of the anti-globalisation movement there was widespread criticism of the multinationals involved in the trainer business, but there was no stopping this all-powerful trio. Much of their success has depended on the technical innovations they have introduced to a product that was no more than a simple rubber sole in the first place. Nike, with its Air Max air-cushion system, represents the ultimate in cushioning; Adidas has its Torsion system for running shoes, which makes the foot much more stable in the shoe; Reebok has the Pump system, inflating the shoe to support the ankle. Puma, New Balance, Vans, Asics and others have also contributed important technical advances and thus helped the evolution of the trainer along. What next? More comfort, improved performance and better design, for a start. At the beginning of the twenty-first century, the sports shoe has irrevocably become an integral part of everyday life.

Details of a trainer: colour contrast and linear play.

2 From changing

-room to cat-walk

The roots
of the phenomenon

It would be wrong to classify trainers as a fashion phenomenon; the way they stormed their way through established dress codes and upset conventions was more radical than that. Nowadays everyone wears trainers, from celebs and top executives to urban guerillas and rappers. Of course, preferences vary according to the wearers' tastes, which may favour either hi-tech, plain or retro models. All the same, the universal nature of trainers remains unchanged. They have had an impact on all ages and all cultures, regardless of sex or ethnic origin. The big brand names are recognised in the four corners of the globe, even in countries comparatively untouched by consumerism.

Although the rise of the celebrity sports star in the 1980s was a major influence on fashion tastes, it was undoubtedly the emergence of Hip Hop that had the greatest effect. More decisively than any other movement, this street culture defined the significance and style of trainers. Streetwear was born. Celebrities could be seen out clubbing, always wearing one or other branded pair of trainers. In the early '90s, the films of American director Spike Lee, and rap groups such as

Public Enemy, Run DMC, LL Cool J, or Soul II Soul, were sources of inspiration for teenagers. The new trainer craze crossed the Atlantic, and the first chain stores devoted solely to trainers rather than to sports equipment in general began to spring up in European capitals. Now twice as many pairs of shoes were sold as in the previous decade, and each season boys and girls, men and women, rushed to scoop up the latest models from the shelves. Although they had been the preserve of teenagers, trainers now became a fashion craze that drew in the older generations – even 30-somethings got the bug. Trainers gradually infiltrated the world of work. In many businesses, often in the new economy, you could find large numbers of young executives in sharply-cut suits with the latest pair of trendy trainers on their feet. It was the culmination of all the social and cultural upheavals of the twentieth century.

Up-to-the-minute trainers

At one time it was fairly simple to find your way through the maze of dress codes. All you had to do was to isolate the specific characteristics of each fashion group, paying special attention to what the 15–25 age group were wearing. Then, things started to get more complicated. Teenagers started mixing-and-matching, wearing a mixture of punk accessories, dungarees or combat trousers, and rapper shoes. Fortunately, sport is still a constant and immense area of inspiration. Recently, for example, trainers inspired by the world of wrestling have started to appear in the shops.

As for brands, Adidas and Nike are still favourites with the young. The German brand, Puma, also has a good reputation for keeping a close eye on trends. Every year, so the experts say, some new label will suddenly loom out of nowhere, because young people aren't easily swayed by advertising. Of course, this worries the multinationals, but they are very resourceful in dealing with these threats. Brands associated with surfers, like Rip Curl, Billabong or Quiksilver, have been able to attract a large public by adapting their products to the high street. Another way to raise your profile is to link in with a celebrity. In 2004 the singer Christina Aguilera was strutting her stuff for Sketchers, and two basketball stars, Steve Francis and Allen Iverson, singers Scarface and Jadakiss, tennis player Venus Williams, and rapper Missy Elliott, signed up with Reebok.

Quite apart from their performance,
the way athletes look is studied
closely by teenagers, who are easily
hooked on what their idols wear.

Trend-setting trainers? Just look at the photo.

In the footsteps of Stan Smith

More than 30 million pairs sold – a world record, according to the *Guinness Book of Records*. The 'Stan Smith' has won over entire generations with its no-nonsense appeal. It was created in 1970 by Horst Dassler, the son and worthy successor of Adi Dassler ('Adi Das-sler'), founder of Adidas. In fact, it was worn initially by the French tennis player, Robert Ayet, whose signature featured below the famous trefoil logo. But then along came American Stan Smith, and he replaced him. Stan Smith was better known (especially after he won Wimbledon) and a much more charismatic individual than Ayet, so the company decided to rename the shoes. The effect was immediate – the 'Stan Smith' became a must-have shoe overnight. Marketing gurus claim that the fantastic success of the 'Stan Smith' marked the start of the public craze for trainers for town wear. Why did it do so well? The 'Stan Smith' represented a considerable advance for its time, as it had leather uppers, whereas most tennis shoes at the time had canvas uppers. Nowadays, who, apart from maybe a few stalwart tennis fans, associates the name Stan Smith with anything more than the name of a legendary shoe? The designer Marc Jacobs, who heads up Louis Vuitton, is never without his 'Stan Smiths', and the same goes for members of the pop groups Air, Cassius and Daft Punk.

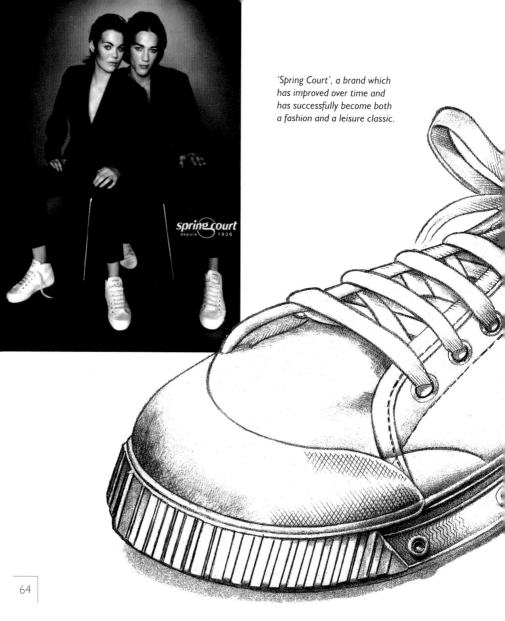

'Spring Court', a brand which has improved over time and has successfully become both a fashion and a leisure classic.

spring court
depuis 1936

The designers step in

Although they can have an influence on streetwear, fashion designers are also prepared to let the street influence them. They adopted trainers, and raised them to the status of fashion icons. The big names in fashion were persuaded to take trainers on to the catwalk – for example, by making them accessories for an evening dress. Models clad in Jean-Paul Gaultier, Vivienne Westwood and Dick Bikkembergs outfits paraded in trainers. Fendi, Dior, Prada, Gucci, Yohji Yamamoto, Christian Lacroix, Marc Jacobs and even Karl Lagerfeld went further, and designed their own versions of trainers. For the favoured few, no wardrobe was complete without a pair of high-fashion trainers.

However, fashion is by its nature always fickle, and before long lesser-known brands eventually emerge to compete with the big three, especially once they have been seen on the feet of some celebrity. Someone will seize on 'Gazelles' because Jamiroquai has been wearing them, or Reebok's 'Hong Kongs'

A still from Runaway Bride *(1999);*
Richard Gere and Julia Roberts wear trainers.

Converse comeback

Jodie Foster, Liv Tyler, Gisèle Bündchen, Mike Myers, Lenny Kravitz, Tommy Lee, Gwyneth Paltrow … the list goes on and on. Apart from being international stars, what do all these celebrities have in common? The answer's quite simple: they are all fans of the famous Converse shoes. The 'Chuck Taylor All Stars' have been in and out of favour over the years, but made a real comeback in the summer of 2002. The 'All-Star' was created in 1917 and was one of the very first shoes designed just for sport. The street didn't latch on to it until the 1950s, when the 'All Star' became an emblem of youth, worn on the big screen by up-and-coming young stars, such as James Dean in *Rebel Without a Cause*. Their popularity continued with films like *West Side Story* and *Grease*, and TV programmes such as *Happy Days* and *Dennis the Menace*. However, in the 1980s Converse lost out to newcomers like Nike, Adidas and Reebok, and to the popularity of their technical improvements. At the end of 2000, Converse was almost bankrupt. Just in time, Converse started to make money again on the back of the retro wave. In recent years the company has had annual sales of almost four million pairs. A snub for Nike? Not really, Nike bought Converse.

Different versions of the famous "Chuck Taylor All Stars", with a very high one shown here, and a Converse design inspired by 1960s and '70s running shoes.

ALL ★ STAR

as worn by Björk, or the 'Mexico 66s' of Onitsuka Tiger (the fashion line of the Japanese manufacturer, Asics). Bruce Lee wore them in his day, and Uma Thurman brought them back into the spotlight in Quentin Tarantino's *Kill Bill (Volume 1)*.

In compliance with the demands of marketing departments, brand manufacturers are quite happy to ask designers to work with them on a model (existing or planned) to be sold as a limited edition. They will do the same when bringing out a new edition of a trainer that has been a bestseller in the past, or with a new model they are convinced is going to be a big hit in the future. (In the case of the latter, however, they will wait for the standard model to take off first). You need to be extremely keen on trainers to buy these limited edition fashion jewels, though; they are often incredibly expensive, some selling for up to £1700!

It's anyone's guess which model is going to catch the public's imagination. People may be as infatuated with the latest technological innovations as with makes they wore when they were kids.

In Quentin Tarantino's film Kill Bill I *(2003), Uma Thurman wears 'Asics' inspired by Bruce Lee's footwear.*

Trainer-casuals: the transformation and development of a cult object. A perfect illustration of how fashion and trainers go together, or of how shoe manufacturers reinterpret fashion for the high street.

Left-hand page:
The rapper Flavor Flav from Public Enemy (big in the 1980s) wearing Fila, very fashionable at the time.

Right-hand page:
Micro jeans and trainers without laces: the latest sexiest outfit.

New Balance: success in Europe

The story of the New Balance '576' is the story of a shoe becoming fashion-able without the assistance of publicity and with the image of a pure sports product. For years, New Balance had been thought of as a brand for mara-thon runners, and then it suddenly acquired cult status. At the end of 1997, the small Boston company hauled 250,000 pairs of old running shoes out of stock. Though unsaleable in the US, the '576's were shipped to Europe. Fashion boutiques and cutting-edge design shops caught on to them, and all of a sudden New Balance was up among the top brands of 2000. Eventually – the real mark of success – hundreds of counterfeit '576's were on sale in cut-price shoe shops.

Puma's 'Clyde', Nike's 'Cortez', Adidas's 'Stan Smiths', Converse's 'All Stars', or New Balance's '576' are all models which have made a startling comeback in our shoe cupboards. Manufacturers generally underplay this fashion aspect of trainers in catalogues and promotional literature, and prefer to stress their sports shoe and sports clothing know-how instead. But their marketing strategies push every angle, and some brands – such as Puma, who gained a new lease of life thanks to this – put considerable emphasis on the fashion element. Trends change regularly; designer models will go retro one season, only to switch next time to martial arts, Formula 1, football, basketball and even boxing style. Adidas brought out versions inspired by Tae Kwondo shoes, with a lace effect. Nike was inspired by the traditional Japanese *tabi* boots (used for martial arts) for one of their summer successes in 2000, their highly-flexible, separated-toe version of Ninja shoes.

A variety of influences has led to a constant mushrooming of new trainer brands, influences often a million miles away from traditional sports goods. Sometimes what is produced

A step closer to fame and glory
under a catwalk spotlight.

A Ralph Lauren sports shoe, somewhere between a trainer and an outdoor shoe.

Nike: a strategy analysed

Shoes at £180. No, that isn't the asking price for a pair at the most expensive shoe boutique in the most expensive shopping district of a big capital city, but simply the high-street price of the latest version of Nike 'Air Jordans'. The 'Jordan Air XVIII' came out in 2003, and cost 'only' about £160. Even the previous year's version cost £125. To launch this latest offering a £9 million budget was allocated to a publicity campaign involving the services of film director Spike Lee. But Americans turned their backs on products like this, which they found far too pricey; teenagers went for much less expensive models, in the £65 to £80 range. This was bad news for the uncontested leader in the sector. Nike hadn't seen the signs; even though key sales outlets sounded the alarm, the manufacturing giant wouldn't listen. The result was a drop in sales – down 3 per cent in 2002 – while their main competitors forged ahead: Reebok was up 8 per cent, Adidas 22 per cent, and Puma a whopping 73 per cent. This must have come as quite a blow to the directors of the company with the 'swoosh' brand! Of course, this small setback doesn't make it any less of a superpower in its field. In the US, Nike still has a 37 per cent market share, and in the rest of the world, with shoe sales to the value of more than £4.5 billion, Nike is way ahead of the others. It remains to be seen whether Nike will demonstrate its ability to adapt to the changing market.

Nike is a brand as familiar as Coca Cola or MacDonald's.

Today this design flies off the shelves. Yesterday it was the latest thing for a would-be champion.

Adidas: goodbye to 'Gazelles'

Do you remember them? In the mid-'90s they were the first to restart the great retro wave that, even today, isn't completely spent. Since then the brand manufacturers haven't stopped delving into their archives in order to sell us legendary models while we're still on this nostalgia kick. In 1993 Australian supermodel Elle MacPherson posed nude in 'Gazelles'. Could any brand want better publicity? Yet Adidas hasn't made them since 2002, a sad end for a successful product, which once featured in a catalogue of top upmarket heritage possessions. 'Gazelles' came off the drawing board of Horst Dassler (yes, that family again) in 1968. They were the ultra-high-tech trainers of their day. Hundreds of thousands of them would be sold in a few months. After an initial three basic colours – black suede, bright red and royal blue – almost 30 other colours were added to the range over a three-year period. But Adidas won't budge, and unfortunately seem determined to concentrate on other niches instead. However, for those who have hung on to their pair, it's a pretty safe bet that in a few years they will be worth a bomb on the vintage clothing market!

is very close to pastiche, a form of town shoe masquerading as a sports trainer. In 1996, Reebok's famous 'Freestyle' was copied by No Box, who turned this feminine dance shoe into a shoe with rubber heels; the town trainer was born. It was targeted at consumers looking for more comfort than in a traditional town shoe, but wanting to avoid something that looked too sport-oriented and laid-back. This approach was responsible for the success of the Spanish Camper brand, who also brought out versions for men as well as women. Other manufacturers copied the concept, and from then on it became a classic shoe category. Versions of trainers with large platform soles were also brought out by No Name, Yellow Cab and even Buffalo. Admittedly, the result wasn't always desperately stylish, but teenagers went for them.

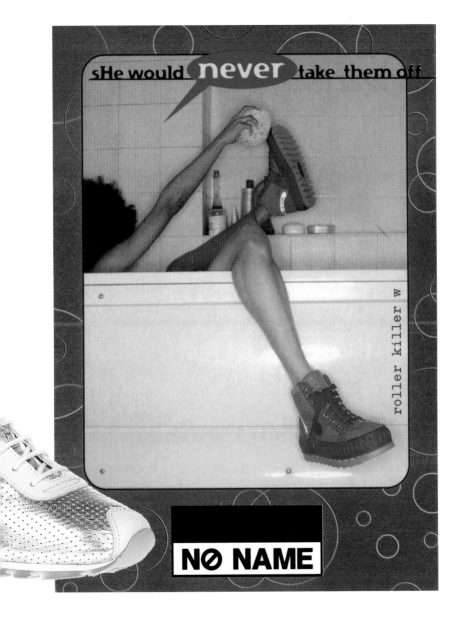

'No-logo' against logos

It's the spitting image of a low-sole version of a Converse, but it's a copy. It doesn't really matter which original it's copying, because what's important here is that it's an example of 'blackSpot sneakers', the activists' trainers with an accusatory black dot. The point is that it wasn't created by one of the big multinationals, but is the work of the magazine *Adbusters*, the voice of anti-globalisation campaigners and other no-logo activists. The aim of these enemies of self-defeating, outdated consumerism is to produce a brand to challenge the famous Converse marque bought by Nike in 2003. For some years now, activists have been turning a critical spotlight on the main producers of sports shoes, who have been accused of exploiting sweatshop workers in developing countries to ensure constantly rising profits. The black dot symbolises the sentence this counterbranding is designed to pass on Nike. Why did Nike take over the makers of the 'Chuck Taylor All Star' rather than some other shoe manufacturer? These militants thought of Converse as a kind of retro-cool, small family business, a type of manufacturer there were now too few of in the US, and one that guaranteed workers a fair wage. They saw Converse's purchase as a declaration of war, and are hoping that the rank outsider they have created in order to oppose Nike will defeat the sports business giant on its own territory.

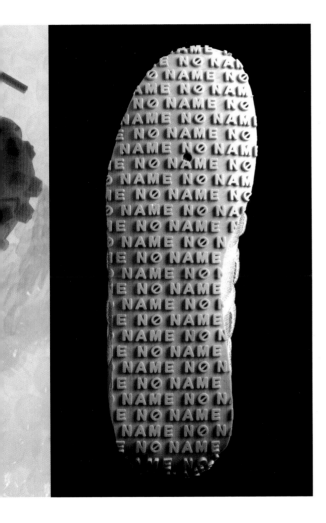

'No Name', a brand marketed by a French shoe manufacturer that made its name with fashion trainers.

Le Coq Sportif: a French comeback

The Americans and Germans have the lion's share of the trainer market. Nevertheless, there is a French label that managed a startling recovery, in the same way that Puma and Converse did. Everyone thought that Le Coq Sportif had finally faded away. Sponsors of the footballer Platini, the cyclist Hinault, and tennis players Yannick Noah and Björn Borg, Coq Sportif has been taken up yet again by the fashion conscious, as sometimes happens with fashion's wheel of fortune. The retro-style 'Wendon', reminiscent of bowling shoes, is back in service. Almost 300,000 pairs were sold in 2001, the first year of its renaissance. This success wasn't a stroke of luck, but the result of a very carefully planned campaign. Stylists reworked lines and colours, with about 10 variations. For the logo, they reverted to the legendary cockerel in a triangle. Finally, the brand opted for a fairly restricted target market (the 'bohemian middle-class', and 'switched-on' wearers), and one very distant from the traditional sports public. After all, like its sister brands, the Coq Sportif is only following fashion. It plans to develop its sports line in order to achieve eminence once again as one of the sector's top manufacturers. The aim is to double turnover and get back into the very exclusive club of 'outsider' brands such as Puma, which will be vital if the label is to survive in the harsh world of fashion.

Which of these would you choose to wear on the starting blocks?

Do you remember when the Spice Girls were always on the radio or on TV? This group of sassy young women, perched on their platforms, had their taste in footwear copied by young girls worldwide.

Another derivative trend was the outdoor, or street-hiking trend; in other words, hiking or hillwalking shoes worn in town. As in the case of town shoes, city dwellers were looking for comfort, combined with a certain ruggedness, possibly with an ecological slant (considered very chic in some new-age circles). In this context, Palladium and Timberland products have appeared on hundreds of feet that will never seek the freedom of the forests or climb the highest peaks, but that will keep instead to the relative safety of city pavements. Surfers and skaters also feed into the trainer melting pot. Brands that have achieved cult status in surfing and skating circles, like Vans, or the once obscure Air Walks, now blossom on non-skaters' feet. This is how fashion works, of course. It is full of contradictions, and determined to mine every seam of a richly varied phenomenon like trainers, which is showing no signs yet of being exhausted.

Even skateboarding trainers haven't been able to escape the latest fashions. Their sharp lines are a major influence on the young.

3 The story of

the brands

Pure nostalgia …

… A high-tech design that (almost) completely sums up a brand's expertise.

Adidas: a one-family reign

The famous cult brand with the three-stripe logo is closely linked to the history of a Bavarian shoemaking family. Adolf ('Adi') Dassler was born in 1901 and soon became a sports enthusiast. He started sewing shoes by hand and this spurred him into producing ready-made footwear for athletics and football. His trainers were worn for the first time at the 1928 Olympic Games in Amsterdam. Adi Dassler felt very involved and looked after 'his' athletes, working closely with them and trying to get the best out of their shoes. At the end of the 1920s, his father Christolf and his brother Rudolf helped him to expand his small business. Adolf was a brilliant inventor. He perfected a system of hand-forged spikes for the soles of track shoes, and had his first success at the 1932 Olympics with Uli Jonath winning a bronze medal in Dassler shoes. Then came the Berlin Olympics, where black American sprinter Jesse Owens won four gold medals. Hitler refused to award him his medals personally, even though Owens was wearing German running shoes.

Adolf Dassler's passionate pursuit of sport took Adidas to the top.

In 1948, Rudolf left the family firm to found Puma. In 1954, Adi was made famous by Adidas removable-stud football boots, which gave Germany World Cup victory. Production rose from 800 to 12,000 pairs a day. During the 1960s, Adidas consolidated its dominant position. In the mid 1970s, more than 75% of NBA basketball players wore Adidas 'Superstars'. At the 1984 Olympics in Los Angeles, 124 of the 140 competing countries wore Adidas footwear. 259 medals were won by athletes wearing the three-stripe logo.

During the next decade Adidas decided to enter the highly competitive American market, in which it would eventually have to witness the rise of its first true rival, Nike. The company had no great successes in the 1980s, and in 1987 Adi died. In order to relaunch the three-leafed Trefoil, the other logo of the brand, a number of changes were successfully instituted, and today Adidas has a major influence both on the young and on the fashion-conscious markets. The 'Adidas Equipment' line, and its optimised cushioning effect, was publicised with the firm's proud assertion that their products were ergonomically based on the design and function of the human foot.

Perfect for stadium or dance floor.

All the technical expertise of a firm put into one famous make that sold by the thousand.

Opposite and following
double-page spread:
*Two versions of a single
model.*

Asics: the up-and-coming Japanese outsider

The only major Japanese brand to have become established at global level was Asics (the initial letters of the Latin tag, *Anima sana in corpore sano*, 'a healthy mind in a healthy body'). The firm was founded in 1949, in a Japan still suffering the effects of World War II, initially under the name of the founder, Kihachiro Onitsuka. In 1951, Asics had its first media success when the winner of the Boston Marathon wore its products. Scientists at the firm developed what was at that time a revolutionary marathon shoe (though now standard practice), thanks to a new vulcanised rubber sole which guaranteed improved cushioning, and vent holes at the tips of the toes. Other innovations were the band supporting the foot arch, and criss-cross support straps on the shoe, which have come to symbolise the brand. In 1986, Asics brought out the invention that would bring it real fame: a unique gel cushioning system. In 2000, the brand launched a new line, 'Onitsuka Tiger', named after the company founder. This collection paid homage to the collectors' pieces of the 1970s and '80s, and answered the call of trainer fans for vintage products.

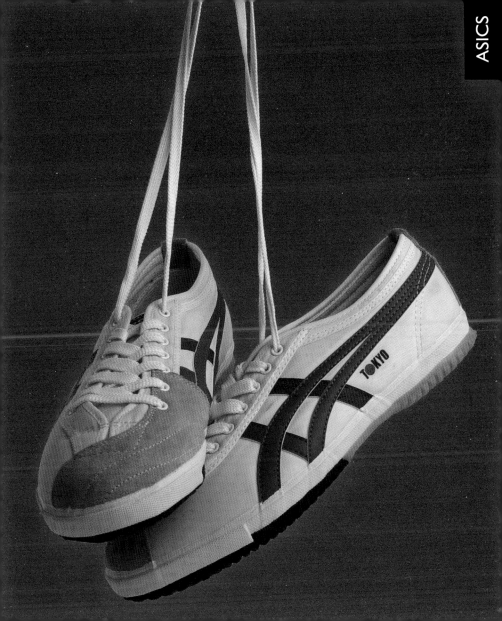

ASICS

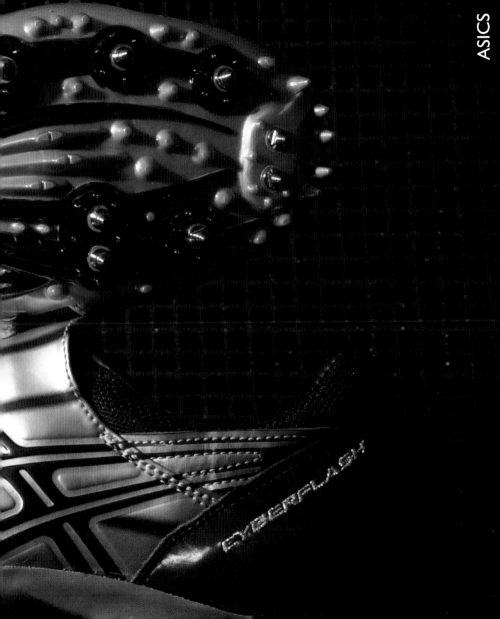

The Japanese firm Asics has been extremely clever with the 'Onitsuka Tiger' range, riding the nostalgia wave by reissuing old 1970s and '80s models – even if they don't impress the ultra-fashion conscious.

Asics helped top athletes smash records with its revolutionary ventilated rubber sole, first in 1951, and then again, with its gel system, in 1986.

Another trendy track-stopper.

A perfect running shoe for a small stride.

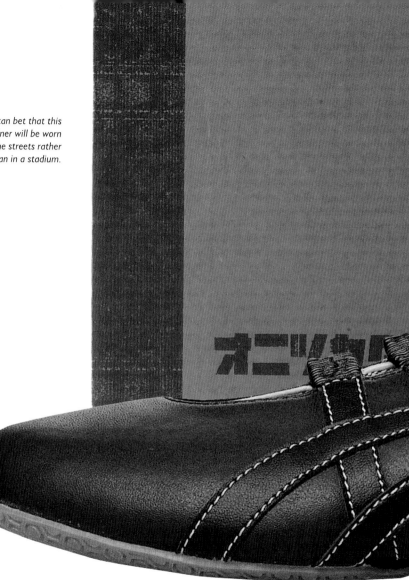

*You can bet that this
trainer will be worn
on the streets rather
than in a stadium.*

Converse: the return of an eternal star

At their very lowest below-par rating, Converse shares were worth no more than 39 cents on the New York Stock Exchange. But that's all in the past, and this American company is now in the best of health. But it was a close shave. The 'All Star', the firm's legendary product, was a has-been. The high-soled boots hadn't stood up to the technology-driven competition of the other major brands in the sector. The company was in deep trouble. In 2000 Converse seemed overwhelmed by debts (of more than £100 million). How had this well-known brand got into such a state? Primarily, because poor management had taken it out of its depth, especially by acquiring a run-down textile company specialising in basketball-related products. Another weak point was the high cost of production: Converse still had its factories in the US, whereas most industrial companies had moved their manufacturing abroad. Converse could no longer afford this luxury, as the terrible results showed. Footwear Acquisition bought Converse at the end of 2001. A draconian downsizing took place, and production was contracted-out to Asia. It looked like there might be no more 'Chuck Taylor All Stars', this famous

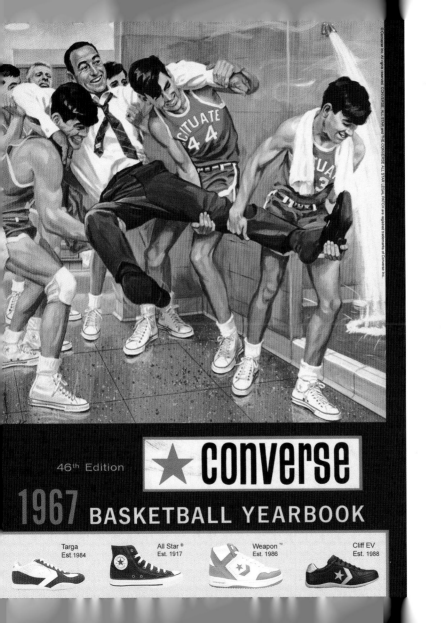

46th Edition

★ converse

1967 BASKETBALL YEARBOOK

Targa
Est. 1984

All Star ®
Est. 1917

Weapon ™
Est. 1986

Cliff EV
Est. 1988

CONVERSE

basketball shoe with its textile upper, created in Massachusetts in 1917. To promote the product, the firm had recruited basketball player Chuck Taylor, the first front man in the history of basketball trainers, and long before Michael Jordan had been signed up to Nike. Driving his Cadillac, he criss-crossed America singing the praises of the canvas shoes. In return, Converse permanently linked his name to that of the 'All Star'. The shoe was highly successful and even acquired cult status during the 1950s, when the 'All Star' became the rebel's shoe. And, 50 years later, even though Converse was losing out badly to the competition, it managed a resounding comeback in spite of the presence of the large multinationals. The 'All Star' had recovered its rebellious image. But this wasn't enough to prevent the Nike, the giant from Oregon, from acquiring this legendary Massachusetts manufacturer. In summer 2003 Nike bought Converse for a meagre $305 million. What did Nike have in mind? It wanted to ensure the continuing success of the 'All Star' which, like jeans, had become a core component of any respectable wardrobe, and to develop the sports clothing side. For Nike, with its top-of-the-range models at prohibitive prices, this was probably a means of positioning itself in a more popular market, and a sensible way of acquiring a broader product range.

Much more than a mere canvas tennis shoe, the 'All Star' has become such a cult object that some people photograph it in each and every version and in ever-newer settings for trainers.

The name Converse also means models specifically designed for sports use, whether tennis, basketball or athletics … although 'Chuck Taylor All Star' fans sometimes forget this.

CONVERSE®

New Balance: quality first

New Balance was founded in 1896, a few miles from Boston. For a long time it remained a small company devoted mainly to the manufacture of orthopaedic shoes and soles. There was nothing exciting about the firm, and nothing to give any hint that one day this brand would be up there competing with the top trainer manufacturers. In 1949, the company entered the world of sport by producing running shoes for overweight people who could not find athletic shoes to cushion their stride. But it was not this minor diversification that really got the firm started; 1972, when six employees were making 30 pairs of shoes a day, was the year things changed in a big way. The arrival of an ambitious and talented individual was to bring about a major alteration in the fortunes of New Balance. Jim Davis, a young engineer of 28, bought the firm for a song – no more than about £50,000. Convinced that interest in ball games was about

A small firm which has now taken on the big players, with a strategy relying on expertise as its major asset.

to explode, Davis rose to the challenge. He created robust yet light, comfortable models which, most importantly of all, took careful account of the anatomy of the foot. Very soon joggers were using them. New Balance was responsible for major innovations in this area; in fact, Davis was the first to offer an integral foam sole, and the only one to provide running shoes with a choice of widths. New Balance would seem to have been the complete antithesis of the other successful brands. There was no question of them falling into the fashion trap, even though the brand had become a benchmark in its own way, almost against its will. All over the world, the fashion conscious have adopted New Balance, although the company has done nothing to encourage this. There are no teams of stylists and designers, no publicity campaigns with major celebrities in hot-air balloons, and no costly sponsoring of top athletes. The firm's slogan sums it up: 'Celebrating athletes with performance driven products.' Another unusual feature is that New Balance shoes are made partly in the US – all in all, not bad going for quite a small firm!

N for New Balance – not the biggest logo, but as tough as they come. A detail of the 576, a major success.

In the 1990s New Balance achieved massive popularity with the 576.

To satisfy everybody the same model is available in different colours and a choice of Velcro or laces. Which one do you go for?

The 577 is the acceptably cool accompaniment for a natty suit worn to the office or a dinner party.

The 832 is the right model for aficionados of sport or fashion. The more high-tech tennis shoes are also much in demand by trendsetters.

They crowd running
tracks and fashionable
trainer stores to get hold
of the RC230.

Nike: absolute masters

Nike is the uncontested Number One and way ahead of its smaller colleagues in the sector, an American company that has become an international brand as well-known as Coca Cola, Levis or even McDonald's. Its amazing history is a genuine American success story. This industrial superpower began with an association in 1957 between Phil Knight, a student at the University of Oregon and a champion runner, and Bill Bowerman, his coach. They both wanted to improve the performance capabilities of sports equipment and decided to put their heads together to look at possible solutions. Knight, by then a student at the Stanford Business School, even created the strategy, in memo form, for a campaign to end the dominant position of Adidas at that time. In 1962, under the name of Blue Ribbon Sport (BRS), he began importing 'Onitsuka Tiger' basketball shoes, made by Kihachiro Onitsuka, the founder of Asics.

In 1967, the pair created the 'Cortez', for marathon runners. It was immediately successful. The 'swoosh' branding was established in 1971. From the start, Nike was anxious to sponsor sportsmen and, setting out to win markets in Europe and South America, relocated its production to Asia. Things took a new turn in 1979 with the astonishing invention of the famous 'Air-Sole'. This air cushioning system was the work of a NASA engineer, Marion Frank Rudy. He had offered his invention to several firms, but only Nike was interested. The principle was simple: cavities, filled with pressurised gas, were created in the sole of the shoe. This new, technology-led approach, catapulted Nike directly to first place in the field. The brand image has been established on an especially elevated level with the sponsorship of top champions like John McEnroe, Carl Lewis, André Agassi, Tiger Woods and Michael Jordan – the front name for a legendary collection of trainers beloved of basketball aficionados. Nike forges ahead and remains at the top thanks to its technical advances, its capacity for renewal and its financial strength.

Some people are prepared to run a marathon
just to get their hands on a super-famous
Nike model. Here is the proof.

NIKE

swatch TIMING

In 1979 Nike brought about a revolution in
the world of sport with its invention of the
air cushioning system, since when 'Air Max'
trainers have become classics. Though well
worn, this pair has been preserved by the
owner with a respect due to sacred objects.

NIKE

A famous trademark
and a four-letter
logo. Do you
recognise me?

NIKE

NIKE

Right-hand page:
Again, a very effective Flower Power version.

Left-hand page:
A reissue of the Cortez, a leading 1970s model.

NIKE

MAYFLY

he ultimate lightweight racing shoe

ould support and cushion you 1 me

ast the finish line before wearing

/e know that for every extra

carry on

use

100km

o the Mayfl

erforman

nginee

unning

n nature t   nsect that

ives, breeds and dies all in one day...

Carpe Diem.

Nike achieved prominence not only through revolutionary processes such as its air cushioning, but also with the help of trainers that have clear, simple lines which somehow still manage to be state-of-the-art, though sometimes with the occasional decorative touch.

Puma:
a big cat's second life

Puma is another brand that has come a long way. In the mid-'90s, the company was close to collapse, and only just avoided filing for bankruptcy. Like Converse, Puma had found it difficult to deal with the unrelenting competition from the big sports corporations. As mentioned, Puma's history is intertwined with that of Adidas. The Dassler brothers decided to go their separate ways, Adi staying with Adidas, and Rudolf founding Puma in 1948. In spite of the somewhat unconventional intra-family competition, neither brother seemed to lose out from the arrangement. Puma made the transition to the US in the 1950s and sponsored athletes there, including Pelé. At the Mexico Olympics in 1968, Tommy Smith and Lee Evans, wearing Pumas, raised their clenched fists on the medal-winners' podium in the Black Power salute. This powerful image would come to typify this particular period in the history of sport. Then came the vicious spiral. In 1994, the company decided it needed a change of strategy in order to continue being successful. To counter the firepower of the big three brands, Puma joined the ranks of firms emphasising

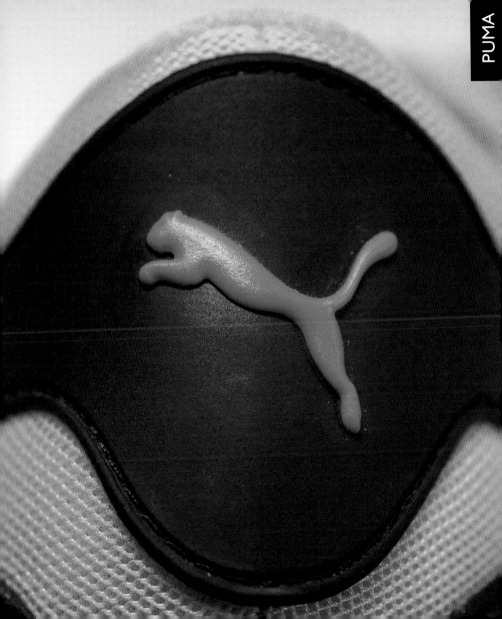

PUMA

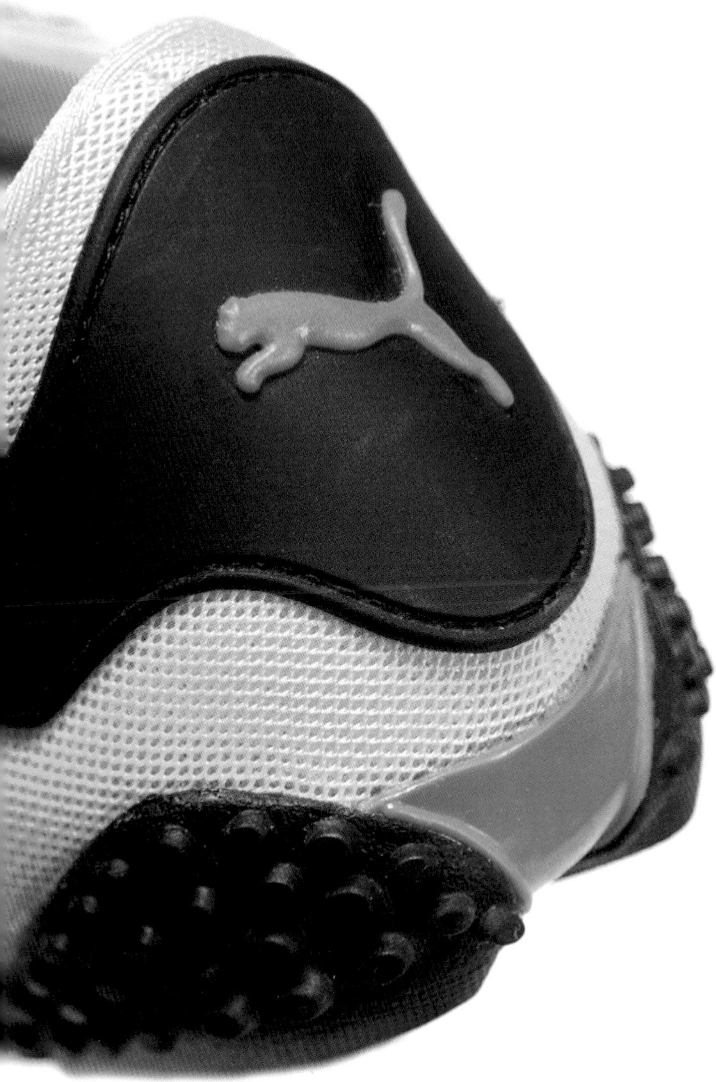

the fashion element of their products, and became the only label to make the craze for basketball-type trainers a strategy in its own right. This was a new marketing concept, and very soon this new approach was to prove profitable. Puma rummaged through its archives for old models to revive in order to feed the craze for retro-look trainers. The 'Clyde' became the sensation of the 1990s. The company was also the first to offer a model in 20 colours. In order to sell its creations, Puma assumed control of its distribution network through trendy boutiques, before opening its own concept stores. To raise the company's profile, Puma increased the number of marketing stunts, as with the most recent craze, the 'Thrift'. This basketball model was issued in a limited edition of exactly 510 pairs, using cloth cut from vintage (ie thrift-store) clothing. Quantities of these numbered pairs were then allocated to around 15 countries. You had to be prepared to pay about £160 to acquire them. Another sales technique has been product placement. Stars are asked – in return for appropriate inducements – to wear Pumas in public. Madonna, Cameron Diaz and Brad Pitt have all been roped in. Thanks to marketing tactics like this, Puma has increased its sales by 55 per cent, and obtains 63 per cent of its turnover from shoe sales alone.

Reebok:
incredible longevity

Who would have believed it? Reebok is the oldest manufacturer of sports or athletic shoes still going. In 1895, Joseph William Foster, a passionate cross-country enthusiast, invented the first studded track shoe. In 1900, he opened his own factory, in which each product was entirely handmade. In 1908, his spiked running pumps were adopted by elite Olympic athletes, and he even offered them custom-made models. After his death his two sons, James and John, took over the company. In 1958 they renamed it Reebok, after the African antelope. Until 1979, Reeboks had not really made much of an impression on the American market, but a sales representative called Paul Fireman decided to change that.

Reebok still manages to punch its weight with the top brands.

In 1982, as a result of his suggestions, Reebok came out with 'Freestyle', one of the first women's performance shoes, and then went ahead with an entire line devoted to dance, aerobic, and keep-fit. This collection eventually made Reebok one of the icons of the '80s. In 1989, Reebok won new glory with the invention of the pump system. This inflatable membrane made a perfect fit around the shape of the foot possible, providing what was at that time an unrivalled degree of support and comfort. Tennis players Michael Chang and Aranxta Sanchez Vicario became the new faces of Reebok by winning the Roland-Garros tournament in 1989 with a little help from the lightweight 'Impulse', the firm's very latest model. In the meantime, ex-sales rep Paul Fireman had become head of a company then worth $900 million in the US alone. In the early 1990s, Reebok tried to recover its Number One position, which had been claimed by Nike. In order to counter the Oregon firm and its association with Michael Jordan, Reebok recruited the rising star of the NBA, Shaquille O'Neal. But the struggle was difficult. Nike remained in front.

The oldest company's expertise has enabled it to keep up in a tough, competitive market.

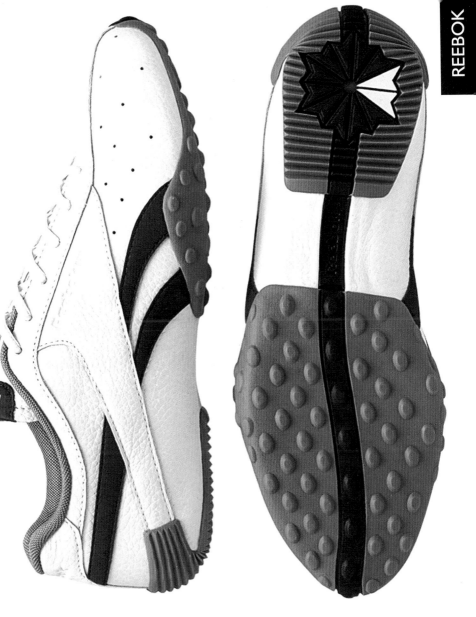

The good old Union Jack manages to win over vast numbers of people far away from its native shores.

The recipe for success for Reebok and its competitors is to mix a suggestion of technical cutting edge with a pinch of design and a hint of the latest fashion.

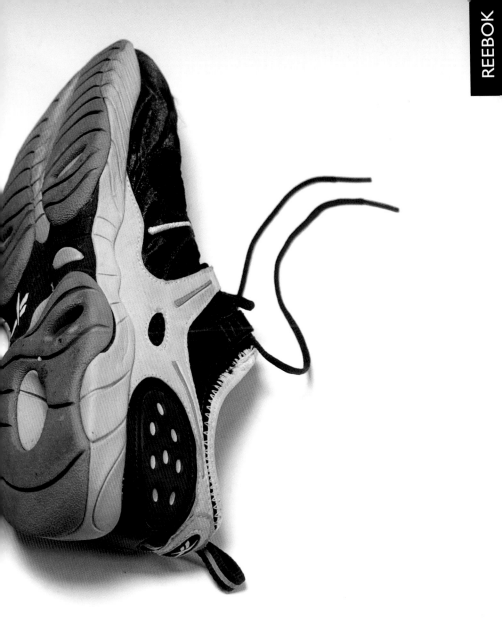

Pony tries to get back into the saddle

Does the name Pony ring a bell? It was an American brand, created in 1972. The single ambition of the proprietor, Roberto Mueller, was to challenge the supremacy of European brands – Adidas in particular. His eminently simple strategy has been to make Pony an alternative to German brands, and this touch of chauvinism in Roberto's motivation launched Pony into orbit. In 1976, he was the only official outfitter for the Montreal Olympics. The following year, at the Super Bowl, the Oakland Raiders, wearing Pony products, beat the Minnesota Vikings. In less than 10 years Roberto Mueller succeeded in getting a quarter of NBA players to wear Pony. The 'wild' style he has adopted, which was the reason for the company's impressive rise to prominence, makes it one of the benchmarks of the age, while still managing to retain the image of an anti-establishment brand. In 1984, Pony generated a turnover of more than a billion dollars across the 40 or so countries in which it is distributed. Worried at this impressive performance, the Dassler family, owners of Puma and Adidas, acquired Pony. However, this tricky three-way marriage led to another sale, to a British group, in 1990. Then the market went into a downturn once again. In 2002, The Firm, a big Hollywood management company, acquired Pony. As result, Dr Dre, Ice Cube, Eminem, Missy Elliott, Method Man, Christina Aguilera, Britney Spears and Tom Cruise were soon to be seen wearing Pony foot gear. Of course the anti-establishment brand of the '70s is going to try the same tactics as Puma and Converse, and try to make a comeback. In an attempt to win the public over again, three collections will soon be invading trendy shop stands and shelves; the archives of Pony designs will be trawled for the styles of the 1970s and '80s; Pony style and Pony performance will place a greater emphasis on design and technical know-how. Will they succeed? It's difficult to say. Sometimes the market that the manufacturers are aiming at can be very fickle.

Pony, an outsider which challenged the big names in the 1970s and '80s, was then consigned to oblivion.

Riding on the back of the nostalgia wave, Pony is trying to make a high-risk comeback by reissuing key models like the 'Mexico 66'.

On your marks!

There are so many other designers' names and manufacturers' labels whose names were once on every tongue. Keds, for example, were created in 1916. These strikingly plain tennis shoes, with white canvas uppers and rubber soles, were the first ones intended for a whole range of leisure activities. They were an undeniable worldwide success, and you can still find hundreds of copies in all the cheaper shoe shops. But who remembers them? There were so many lookalikes that the name got buried. Fashion has the ability to make and destroy brands by attaching them to a specific era. L.A. Gear, the leading children's basketball shoe manufacturer, had its heyday in the 1980s, thanks to its customised range, but today no one would dream of wearing them. The same goes for Fila, the Italian brand that then became American, which achieved cult status in the 1990s. It was the same with Lotto, another Italian label, which was worn in 1985 by the sports personalities of the day: Boris Becker, Martina Navratilova and Ruud Gullit. Vans, with its no-lace model, was a fantastic success; it has managed to keep the brand among the top 10 manufacturers, even if its fashion image is somewhat scuffed. Fortunately, some brands, like Spring Court and Superga, improve with time and become major classics.

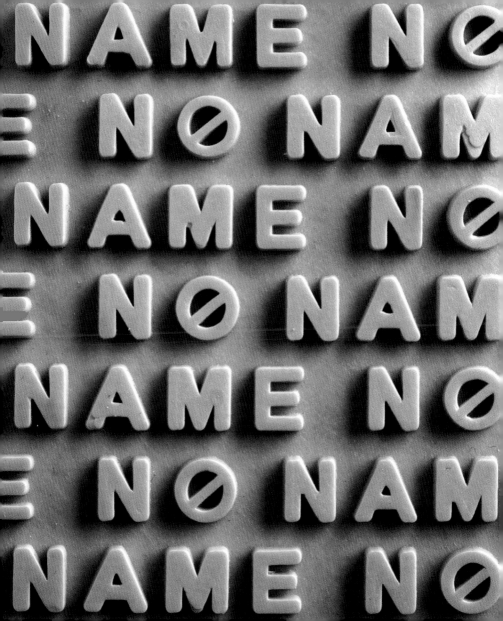